HOCKEY

Megan Kopp
and Aaron Carr

MEDIA ENHANCED BOOKS
AV2 BY WEIGL™
ADDED VALUE • AUDIO VISUAL

www.av2books.com

AV² provides enriched content that supplements and complements this book. Weigl's AV² books strive to create inspired learning and engage young minds in a total learning experience.

Your AV² Media Enhanced books come alive with...

Audio
Listen to sections of the book read aloud.

Video
Watch informative video clips.

Embedded Weblinks
Gain additional information for research.

Try This!
Complete activities and hands-on experiments.

Key Words
Study vocabulary, and complete a matching word activity.

Quizzes
Test your knowledge.

Slide Show
View images and captions, and prepare a presentation.

... and much, much more!

Go to **www.av2books.com**, and enter this book's unique code.

BOOK CODE

Z 6 3 3 9 1 2

AV² by Weigl brings you media enhanced books that support active learning.

Published by AV² by Weigl
350 5ᵗʰ Avenue, 59ᵗʰ Floor
New York, NY 10118
Website: www.av2books.com   www.weigl.com

Library of Congress Cataloging-in-Publication Data

Kopp, Megan.
 Hockey / Megan Kopp and Aaron Carr.
   p. cm. -- (The greatest)
 Includes bibliographical references and index.
 ISBN 978-1-61690-701-3 (hardcover : alk. paper) -- ISBN 978-1-61690-706-8 (softcover : alk. paper)
1. Hockey--Juvenile literature. I. Carr, Aaron. II. Title.
 GV847.25.K66 2012
 796.962--dc22
                          2011002314

Printed in the United States of America in North Mankato, Minnesota
1 2 3 4 5 6 7 8 9 0 15 14 13 12 11

062011
WEP290411

Project Coordinator Aaron Carr
Art Director Terry Paulhus

Photo Credits
Every reasonable effort has been made to trace ownership and to obtain permission to reprint copyright material. The publishers would be pleased to have any errors or omissions brought to their attention so that they may be corrected in subsequent printings.

Weigl acknowledges Getty Images as its primary image supplier for this title.

Contents

3

Introduction

The world of professional sports has a long history of great moments. The most memorable moments often come when the sport's greatest players overcome their most challenging obstacles. For the fans, these moments come to define their favorite sport. For the players, they stand as a measuring post of success.

As one of the oldest professional sports in North America, hockey has a long history that is filled with great players and great moments. These moments include Wayne Gretzky scoring 50 goals in just 39 games and Mark Messier leading the New York Rangers to their first Stanley Cup championship in 54 years. Hockey has no shortage of such moments, when the sport's brightest stars accomplished feats that ensured they would be forever remembered as the greatest players.

Mark Messier was one of hockey's greatest players.

Training Camp

Hockey is played with 12 players on the ice at a time. Both teams have three forwards, including a center, a left winger, and a right winger. There are also two defensemen and a goaltender on each team. The goaltender, or goalie, defends the team's net. The defensemen help the goalie defend against goals, and the forwards try to score goals.

The Hockey Rink

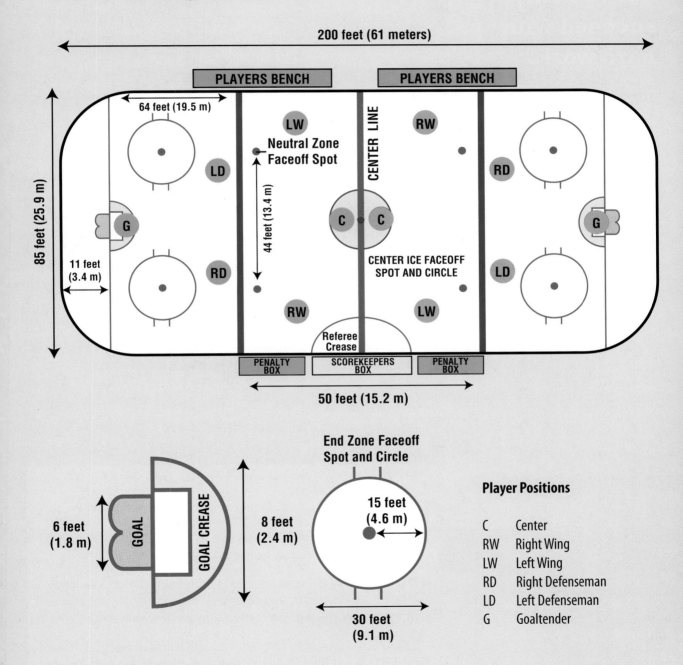

200 feet (61 meters)

PLAYERS BENCH   PLAYERS BENCH

64 feet (19.5 m)

LW

CENTER LINE

RW

Neutral Zone
Faceoff Spot

LD

RD

44 feet (13.4 m)

85 feet (25.9 m)

G

C   C

G

11 feet
(3.4 m)

RD

CENTER ICE FACEOFF
SPOT AND CIRCLE

LD

RW

LW

Referee
Crease

PENALTY
BOX

SCOREKEEPERS
BOX

PENALTY
BOX

50 feet (15.2 m)

End Zone Faceoff
Spot and Circle

GOAL CREASE

GOAL

6 feet
(1.8 m)

8 feet
(2.4 m)

15 feet
(4.6 m)

30 feet
(9.1 m)

Player Positions

C   Center
RW   Right Wing
LW   Left Wing
RD   Right Defenseman
LD   Left Defenseman
G   Goaltender

> **"Talent is a gift from God, but you only succeed with hard work."**
>
> Jean Béliveau

As captain of the Montreal Canadiens, Jean Béliveau led his team to five Stanley Cup championships. No other player has captained his team to more championships.

Player Profile

BORN Jean Arthur Béliveau was born August 31, 1931, in Trois Rivières, Quebec, Canada.

FAMILY Béliveau was one of Arthur and Laurette Béliveau's seven children. He had four brothers and two sisters. Béliveau married Elise Couture in 1953. The couple had one daughter, Helene.

EDUCATION Béliveau attended L'École Saint-David, L'Academie Saint-Louis de Gonzague, and Collége de Victoriaville. He was awarded an honorary degree in physical education from the University of Moncton.

AWARDS Ten-time Stanley Cup champion, 1956 **Art Ross Trophy** winner, two-time **Hart Memorial Trophy** winner, 1965 **Conn Smythe Trophy,** 14 all-star selections, 1964 all-star game **Most Valuable Player (MVP),** inducted into the Hockey Hall of Fame in 1972, 2009 NHL Lifetime Achievement Award winner

Jean Béliveau
Center

Early Years

Jean Béliveau was born and raised in Quebec. As a child, he played hockey with his family and friends in his family's backyard ice rink. When Béliveau was 12, he started playing organized hockey. By age 15, he was playing for the Quebec Aces in the senior league.

In 1951, Béliveau played two games with the Montreal Canadiens. By the 1953–1954 season, the 6-foot, 3-inch tall, 205-pound center joined the National Hockey League (NHL). He played his entire hockey career in Quebec.

Developing Skills

Béliveau was a powerful skater and a natural leader. He was admired by fans, teammates, and opposing players alike. Béliveau soon became one of the league's best players. In just his fourth season with the Canadiens, he was the NHL's top scorer and was named league MVP.

In Montreal, Béliveau won the Stanley Cup 10 times. This is second only to Henry Richard, who won the cup 11 times. For the last 10 seasons of his career with the Canadiens, Béliveau was the team captain.

In total, Béliveau played 20 seasons in the NHL. He recorded 507 goals in the regular season and 79 playoff goals. He added to these numbers with a total of 809 **assists**. In 1971, Béliveau retired as the fourth player in NHL history to score 500 goals. He was Montreal's all-time leader in points and second all-time in goals. Béliveau retired as the NHL's all-time leading playoff scorer.

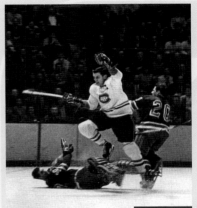

Jean Béliveau

Greatest Moment

In game 7 of the 1965 Stanley Cup finals, the Montreal Canadiens skated to a 4–0 victory over the Chicago Blackhawks. It was Béliveau's first championship as team captain. He scored eight goals and eight assists in 13 playoff games. The win was also important because it was first time the Canadiens won the Stanley Cup since Maurice "The Rocket" Richard retired in 1960. Béliveau took over as team captain after Richard retired, and he faced much criticism when the team did not win. Béliveau later became known as one of the greatest captains in the team's history.

Jean Béliveau holds the NHL record for most Stanley Cup wins. In addition to his 10 wins as a player, Béliveau won another seven Stanley Cups as a team executive.

> ## "My competitive juices are starting to flow again."

Phil Esposito

Phil Esposito scored 118 game-winning goals throughout his career. This is a record that is still unbroken.

Player Profile

BORN Philip Anthony Esposito was born on February 20, 1942, in Sault Ste. Marie, Ontario, Canada.

FAMILY Esposito is the oldest of two sons born to Patrick and Frances Esposito. His brother, Tony, was one of hockey's greatest goalies.

EDUCATION Esposito attended high school but did not graduate.

AWARDS Two-time Stanley Cup champion, Five-time Art Ross Trophy winner, two-time Hart Memorial Trophy winner, two-time **Lester B. Pearson Award** winner, 1978 Lester Patrick Trophy for service to hockey in the United States, 1972 Lou Marsh trophy as Canadian Athlete of the Year, 12 all-star selections, inducted into the Hockey Hall of Fame in 1984

Phil Esposito
Center

Early Years

Phil Esposito and his younger brother, Tony, played hockey in their basement using a rolled up sock for a puck. Being older, Esposito took the shots, and Tony played goalie. The pair often loaded a sled with hockey gear and hauled it to the ice rink at 4:30 or 5:00 in the morning for practice.

Even so, Esposito did not take hockey too seriously. At age 12, he did not make the local bantam team. His skating skills were not good enough. Luckily, Esposito was confident, strong, and had a knack for scoring. He kept playing, even when he had a hard time breaking into the NHL. He played for the St. Louis Braves in the Central Hockey League from 1962 to 1964. In his first year with the Braves, he scored 90 points in 71 games. In his second year, he scored 80 points in 43 games. Finally, the Chicago Blackhawks called him up.

Developing Skills

After a few years in the minors, Esposito joined the Chicago Blackhawks in 1963. Four years later, he was traded to the Boston Bruins, where he was teamed with defenseman Bobby Orr. In 1969, he became the first player in NHL history to score 100 points in a season. That year, Esposito recorded 126 points. He scored more than 100 points in a season five more times, including 152 points in 1970–1971.

Phil was never known to be a quick skater, but the 5-foot, 10-inch tall center knew how to pass and how to score. He often filled the opposing team's **crease** with his body and scored before anyone knew he had the puck. Esposito played his final years with the New York Rangers. He played a total of 18 seasons in the NHL.

Phil Esposito

Greatest Moment

The 1970–1971 season was magic for Esposito. He had an incredible 550 shots on goal. This is a record that remains unbroken. With the numbers on his side, he scored a total of 76 goals, breaking Bobby Hull's record for the most goals in a single season. He also added 76 assists to set a new record for most points in a season, with 152. His goal-scoring record stood for more than 10 years, until Wayne Gretzky's record-smashing 1981–1982 NHL season.

When Phil Esposito retired in 1981, he was the second leading all-time scorer in the NHL for both goals and points. Only Gordie Howe had scored more.

> ## "You miss 100 percent of the shots you don't take."
>
> Wayne Gretzky

Wayne Gretzky is often called "The Great One." He is considered the greatest hockey player of all time. His jersey number, 99, has been retired by all teams in the NHL.

Player Profile

BORN Wayne Douglas Gretzky was born on January 26, 1961, in Brantford, Ontario, Canada.

FAMILY Gretzky is the oldest of five children born to Phyllis and Walter Gretzky.

EDUCATION Wayne attended Sir James Dunne Collegiate and Vocational School, but he did not graduate. He left early to pursue his career in hockey.

AWARDS Four-time Stanley Cup champion, nine-time Hart Memorial Trophy winner, 10-time Art Ross Trophy winner, two-time Conn Smythe Trophy winner, five-time Lester B. Pearson Trophy winner, five-time **Lady Byng Memorial Trophy** winner, 1994 Lester Patrick Trophy for service to hockey in the United States, 18 all-star selections, three-time all-star game MVP, inducted into the Hockey Hall of Fame in 1999

Wayne Gretzky
Center

Early Years

Gretzky put on his first pair of skates when he was two years old. By age six, he was spending every spare moment skating in the backyard rink his dad built. Gretzky's dad was his first hockey coach. He told Gretzky not to skate to where the puck is, but to skate to where the puck will be.

Gretzky started playing organized hockey at age six. He was too good to play with kids his own age. He played against 10-year-olds instead. His jersey was too big for him, so he tucked one side into his pants. This later became a trademark that he continued throughout his career. By the time Gretzky was 11, he collected 517 points in one season.

Developing Skills

In his first full year in the NHL, Gretzky tied Marcel Dionne for the league lead in scoring. Dionne scored more goals than Gretzky, so he won the Art Ross Trophy. Gretzky could not win Rookie of the Year because he had played in the World Hockey Association (WHA) the year before. The NHL did not consider WHA players to be rookies. However, at age 18, he became the only first-year player ever to win the Hart Memorial Trophy.

The following year, Gretzky won his first of seven straight league scoring titles. He also broke Bobby Orr's record for most assists in a season. The year after that, he beat Phil Esposito's record for goals in a season when he netted the puck 92 times.

The records kept breaking, and victory came to both Gretzky and the Oilers. The team won four Stanley Cup championships in five years. When he retired in 1999, Gretzky held 61 NHL records.

Wayne Gretzky

Greatest Moment

Gretzky has been called the greatest hockey player of all time. Throughout his career, he broke and re-broke records many times.

Perhaps the greatest moments for Gretzky were when he surpassed the records set by his childhood hero, Gordie Howe. Growing up, Gretzky always wore number 9, like Howe. One year, that number was already taken, so he settled for 99 instead.

Gretzky went on to break Howe's record of 1,850 career points in 1989. He then passed Howe's record of 801 career goals in 1994. In 1999, he retired with records for most career goals (894), assists (1,963), and points (2,857).

In his final NHL season, Gretzky broke one last record. He scored his 1,072nd career goal, including regular season and playoffs in both the NHL and WHA. This put him ahead of Gordie Howe by one goal.

> **"You find that you have peace of mind and can enjoy yourself, get more sleep, and rest when you know that it was a 100 percent effort that you gave– win or lose."**
>
> Gordie Howe

Gordie Howe is known by many as "Mr. Hockey." He finished in the top five in NHL scoring for 20 straight seasons.

Player Profile

BORN Gordon "Gordie" Howe was born on March 31, 1928, in Floral, Saskatchewan, Canada.

FAMILY Howe is the sixth of Ab and Catherine Howe's nine children. In 1953, Howe married Colleen Joffa. She was the first female manager in hockey. The couple had four children, Marty, Mark, Cathy, and Murray.

EDUCATION Howe attended school until the eighth grade before leaving to pursue a career in hockey. In 2010, he was awarded an honorary doctorate degree from the University of Saskatchewan.

AWARDS Four-time Stanley Cup champion, six-time Art Ross Trophy winner, six-time Hart Memorial Trophy winner, 1967 Lester Patrick Trophy for service to hockey in the United States, 23 all-star selections, 1965 all-star game MVP, inducted into the Hockey Hall of Fame in 1972, 2008 NHL Lifetime Achievement Award

Gordie Howe
Right Wing

Early Years

At age five, Howe received a pair of secondhand skates. He spent hours skating on frozen ponds. Three years later, Howe started playing organized hockey. In 1942, Howe attended a New York Rangers training camp as a 15-year-old. He ended up returning home before the end of the camp. The following year, Howe started playing for the Detroit Red Wings' junior team. Although he only scored seven goals in his rookie season, his strength and abilities caught people's attention. In 1946, Howe started playing with the Detroit Red Wings in the NHL. He was only 18 years old.

Developing Skills

Howe quickly became a star in the NHL. He matched speed and stick-handling with strength and toughness. However, his secret weapon was his ability to shoot equally well left- or right-handed.

Howe formed the famous "Production Line" with Hall of Famers Sid Abel and Ted Lindsay. The trio dominated play with their scoring ability. In 1950, the trio finished the season ranked first, second, and third in league scoring. Howe retired in 1971. However, he joined WHA's Houston Aeros in 1973. Howe later came back to the NHL with the Hartford Whalers. When he retired for a second time, he was 52 years old.

In total, Howe played 1,767 regular season and 157 playoff games in the NHL. In regular season play, he scored 801 goals and 1,049 assists, for a total of 1,850 points. He ranks second all-time in career goals and third all-time in career points. Between the NHL and WHA, Howe scored 975 career regular season goals. This is a record that even Wayne Gretzky did not break.

Gordie Howe

Greatest Moment

In the course of his great career, Howe set and broke many records. At the time of his retirement, he held all of the major NHL scoring records.

Howe's greatest moment, however, may have been when he joined his sons Mark and Marty on the Houston Aeros of the WHA. At age 45, Howe played on the same line as his two sons. In his first year with the team, Howe was named MVP and Mark received the Rookie of the Year award. Howe and his sons helped the Aeros win the WHA championship that year. The following year, the WHA's MVP award was renamed the Gordie Howe Award.

In 1997, Gordie Howe played one game in the International Hockey League. This made him the first player to play on a professional team in six different decades.

"My coach came up to me and said, 'Do you want to be a goalie or forward this year?' It was the biggest decision of my life, and I was seven years old. I don't know why I decided, but I thought it would be fun to play goal."

Martin Brodeur

Martin Brodeur is one of the most dominant goaltenders in the history of the NHL. During his 19-year career, he has broken nearly every record for a goaltender.

Player Profile

BORN Martin Pierre Brodeur was born on May 6, 1972, in Montreal, Quebec.

FAMILY Brodeur is the youngest of Denis and Mireille Brodeur's five children. He has two brothers and two sisters. Brodeur is married and has five children, four sons and one daughter.

EDUCATION Brodeur graduated from high school in St. Leonard.

AWARDS Three-time Stanley Cup champion, five-time William M. Jennings Trophy winner for allowing the fewest goals against in the regular season, four-time Vezina Trophy winner as the NHL's best goaltender, 1994 **Calder Memorial Trophy** winner, two-time Olympic gold medalist, 10 all-star selections

Martin Brodeur
Goaltender

Early Years

Martin Brodeur was four years old when he first tried skating. By age six, he was playing forward in an organized hockey league. When his older brother's team needed a backup goalie for a tournament, Brodeur filled the position. At age seven, Brodeur's coach asked him which position he wanted to play. He chose goalie. He played in the Saint-Leonard Minor Hockey Association until he was 15, when he joined the Montreal Bourassa AAA midget team. In 1989, he was drafted by the Quebec **Major Junior** League, to play for the Saint-Hyacinthe Laser. A year later, Brodeur was drafted by the New Jersey Devils of the NHL.

Developing Skills

In the 1991–1992 season, Brodeur was only called up to the NHL four times as relief for injured goaltenders. His first NHL game, against the Boston Bruins, was a 4–2 win. Brodeur played his first full NHL season in 1993–1994. He was awarded the Calder Trophy as the league's top rookie. The following season, Brodeur and his team won the Stanley Cup. It was a first not only for Brodeur but for the New Jersey Devils as well.

Brodeur holds almost every major NHL record for a goaltender. At the end of the 2010–2011 season, he held 23 NHL records for goaltenders. He is the NHL's all-time leader in regular-season wins (625), **shutouts** (116), and games played (1,132). Brodeur is tied with Patrick Roy for the all-time playoff shutout lead, with 23. This includes a record seven shutouts in the 2002–2003 playoffs alone. His 48 wins in a season is another all-time best.

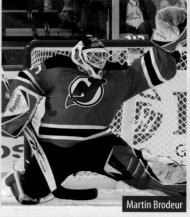

Martin Brodeur

Greatest Moment

Brodeur has experienced many great moments throughout his career. One of his greatest moments came on December 21, 2009. In a game against the Pittsburgh Penguins, Brodeur stopped all 35 shots he faced to break the NHL all-time shutout record. Terry Sawchuk's record of 103 career shutouts had stood for more than 45 years. By breaking the shutout record, Brodeur had added the last remaining all-time NHL goaltending record to his already impressive list of accomplishments.

Martin Brodeur is the only NHL goalie to score a game-winning goal. He is also one of only two goalies ever to score a goal in both the regular season and the playoffs.

> **"I think we have to show some pride in the jersey that we are wearing, and can't quit."**
>
> Mario Lemieux

Mario Lemieux is one of the best players in the history of the NHL. It is fitting, then, that the name "Lemieux" is French for "the best."

Player Profile

BORN Mario Lemieux was born on October 5, 1965, in Montreal, Quebec, Canada.

FAMILY Lemieux is the youngest of three boys born to Pierrette and Jean-Guy Lemieux. Jean-Guy was a construction worker. Lemieux's brother, Alain, also played in the NHL. Lemieux married Nathalie Asselin in 1993. The couple have four children.

EDUCATION Lemieux attended high school but did not graduate. He left school at age 16 to focus on hockey.

AWARDS Two-time Stanley Cup champion, six-time Art Ross Trophy winner, three time Hart Memorial Trophy winner, four-time Lester B. Pearson Award winner, two-time Conn Smythe Trophy winner, 1985 Calder Trophy winner, 1993 **Bill Masterton Memorial Trophy** winner, 2000 Lester Patrick Trophy for service to hockey in the United States, 2002 Olympic gold medal, 10 all-star selections, three-time all-star game MVP, inducted into the Hockey Hall of Fame in 1997

Mario Lemieux
Center

Early Years

Mario Lemieux was skating at age two. At age six, he was playing organized hockey. Lemieux played for Canada in the 1983 World Junior Championships.

From 1981 to 1984, he played major junior hockey in Laval, Quebec. During this time, he was named player of the year for all major junior players. In his last year in major junior, Lemieux beat Guy Lafleur's record for most goals in one season. That season, he scored 133 goals in 70 games to break the record of his childhood hero.

Developing Skills

Lemieux scored his first NHL goal in 1984. He scored in his first NHL game with the first shot he took. He went on to record 100 points in his rookie season. In 1988–1989, the 6-foot, 4-inch tall, 230-pound center tallied 85 goals and 199 points. It was his best single season performance.

Lemieux spent 17 seasons with the Pittsburgh Penguins. He led the team to back-to-back Stanley Cup championships in 1991 and 1992. In total, he played 915 games in the NHL, scoring 690 goals and 1,033 assists for 1,723 points in regular season play. These numbers are even more impressive considering the fact that back injuries kept Lemieux from ever playing a full season. In 1993, he was diagnosed with cancer. "Super Mario" missed two months of the season but still won the scoring title, with 69 goals and 160 points in just 60 games played.

Lemieux retired in 1997. However, he came back in the 2000–2001 season. In 2006, health problems forced him to retire again.

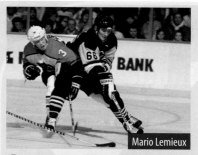
Mario Lemieux

Greatest Moment

On New Year's Eve, 1988, Lemieux accomplished a record that no other player before or since has been able to achieve. In a game against the New Jersey Devils, Lemieux scored five goals. This would be good in itself, but he scored the goals in five different ways. Lemieux had one regular goal with full teams on either side. He also had a **power play** goal, a **short-handed** goal, a **penalty shot** goal, and an empty-net goal.

Mario Lemieux was one of the most dangerous penalty killers of all time. He holds the NHL records for most short-handed goals in a season, with 13.

"I came into the league as a fourth-line grinder that played a limited role."

Mark Messier

Mark Messier is considered one of the greatest leaders in sports history. He is the only person in any professional sport to captain two different teams to league championships.

Player Profile

BORN Mark John Douglas Messier was born on January 18, 1961, in Edmonton, Alberta, Canada.

FAMILY Douglas and Mary-Jean Messier had two sons, Mark and Paul. Douglas was a minor league hockey player and coach. Messier's older brother also played in the NHL. Messier is married and has three children.

EDUCATION Messier left Edmonton's St. Xavier High School before graduating in order to pursue a hockey career.

AWARDS Six-time Stanley Cup champion, two-time Hart Memorial Trophy winner, two-time Lester B. Pearson Award winner, 1984 Conn Smythe Trophy winner, 15 all-star selections, inducted into the Hockey Hall of Fame in 2007

Mark Messier
Left-Wing/Center

Early Years

Growing up in a hockey family, it was only natural that Messier started playing hockey at a young age. He was watching his father's minor-league practices at age four. The next year, Messier started playing organized hockey.

Messier started playing junior hockey for the Spruce Grove Mets at age 15. By age 16, Messier weighed about 200 pounds. His size earned him the nickname, "The Moose." Messier left junior hockey early and joined the Indianapolis Racers of the WHA. He was 17 years old. The Racers had given Messier a five-game tryout, but the team soon folded. Messier then joined the Cincinnati Stingers for the rest of the 1978–1979 season. He played 47 games, recorded one goal and 10 assists, and added 58 penalty minutes.

Developing Skills

In 1979, Messier was drafted by the Edmonton Oilers. In just a few short years, he was scoring more than 100 points per season playing with Wayne Gretzky. When the Oilers won the Stanley Cup in 1984, Messier was named playoff MVP. Though Gretzky finished the playoffs with more points, Messier's leadership earned him the award.

Messier became captain of the Oilers when Gretzky was traded to the Los Angeles Kings in 1988. Messier scored a career high 129 points in 1990. That year, the Oilers won the Stanley Cup.

Messier played 25 seasons in the NHL. His career total of 1,887 points is second only to Gretzky. He also ranks third all-time in assists (1,193) and seventh all-time in goals (694).

Mark Messier

Greatest Moment

In a career full of great moments, one of Messier's best came in the 1993–1994 season. It was a best-of-seven series for the Eastern Conference title. The winner would go on to play for the Stanley Cup. Messier and the New York Rangers were trailing the New Jersey Devils three games to two.

Messier told reporters that the Rangers would win game 6. He guaranteed the victory. Messier then scored a **hat trick** in the third period to win the game. The Rangers also won game 7. In the Stanley Cup final against the Vancouver Canucks, the series went the full seven games. In game 7, Messier scored the game-winning goal. It was the first time in 54 years that the New York Rangers won the cup.

Mark Messier had one of the longest careers in NHL history. In his 25 seasons, he played in 1,756 games. Only Gordie Howe has played in more games.

> "I'm really no different than anybody else, except that sometimes I get my name in the paper."

Bobby Orr

Bobby Orr is considered the greatest defenseman of all time. He won the James Norris Trophy as the league's top defender eight years in a row. This is an accomplishment no other player has ever achieved.

Player Profile

BORN Robert Gordon Orr was born on March 20, 1948, in Parry Sound, Ontario, Canada.

FAMILY Orr is the third of five children born to Alva and Doug Orr. He had two brothers and two sisters. Orr is married and has two sons.

EDUCATION Orr attended R.S. McLaughlin Collegiate but did not graduate. He left early to pursue a career in hockey.

AWARDS Two-time Stanley Cup champion, eight-time **James Norris Trophy** winner, two-time Art Ross Trophy winner, three-time Hart Memorial Trophy winner, two-time Conn Smythe Trophy winner, 1967 Calder Trophy winner, 1975 Lester B. Pearson Award winner, 1979 Lester Patrick Trophy for service to hockey in the United States, nine all-star selections, 1972 all-star game MVP, inducted into the Hockey Hall of Fame in 1979

Bobby Orr
Defense

Early Years

Bobby Orr's first pair of skates came from a family friend. He was four years old. The skates were so big that he needed to stuff paper in the toes to keep them from falling off. One year later, he played his first year of organized hockey. Orr was smaller than many of the other kids, but he could skate faster than anyone his age.

Orr first caught the attention of a scout for the Boston Bruins in 1960. At the time, Orr was as a 12-year-old defenseman playing in a tournament. At age 14, he signed a contract to play with the Oshawa Generals of the Ontario Hockey League (OHL). His 94 points in the 1965–1966 season set a new record for poins by an OHL defenseman.

Developing Skills

When Orr was 18 years old, he joined the NHL with the Boston Bruins. In his first season, Orr scored 41 points and was named rookie of the year. In 1970, Orr was awarded the Art Ross Trophy. He is the only defenseman ever to lead the NHL in scoring. That year, the Bruins won their first Stanley Cup in 29 years. In 1970–1971, Orr had his best season, recording 37 goals and 102 assists. His 139 points is a record that still stands. It is the most points ever scored by a defenseman in a single season.

Orr played only 12 seasons in the NHL, splitting his career between the Bruins and the Chicago Blackhawks. He scored more than 100 points in a season six times. When Orr retired, he held 12 NHL records, including most points, assists, and goals in a season by a defenseman. Knee injuries cut his career short.

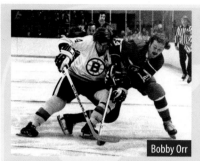

Bobby Orr

Greatest Moment

Bobby Orr's greatest moment has become one of the best-known moments in hockey history. In the 1970 Stanley Cup final between the Boston Bruins and St. Louis Blues, Orr scored the championship-winning goal in overtime to earn the Bruins their first Stanley Cup title in 29 years.

The Bruins skated to easy victories in the first three games of the series. In game 4, however, the two teams battled to a 3–3 tie at the end of the third period. In overtime, Orr received a pass and broke for the net. He shot the puck and scored just as he was being tripped by a defending player. Orr was flying through the air when he saw the puck go in the net.

Bobby Orr retired in 1979 at the age of 31. That year, he became the youngest player in history to be inducted into the Hockey Hall of Fame.

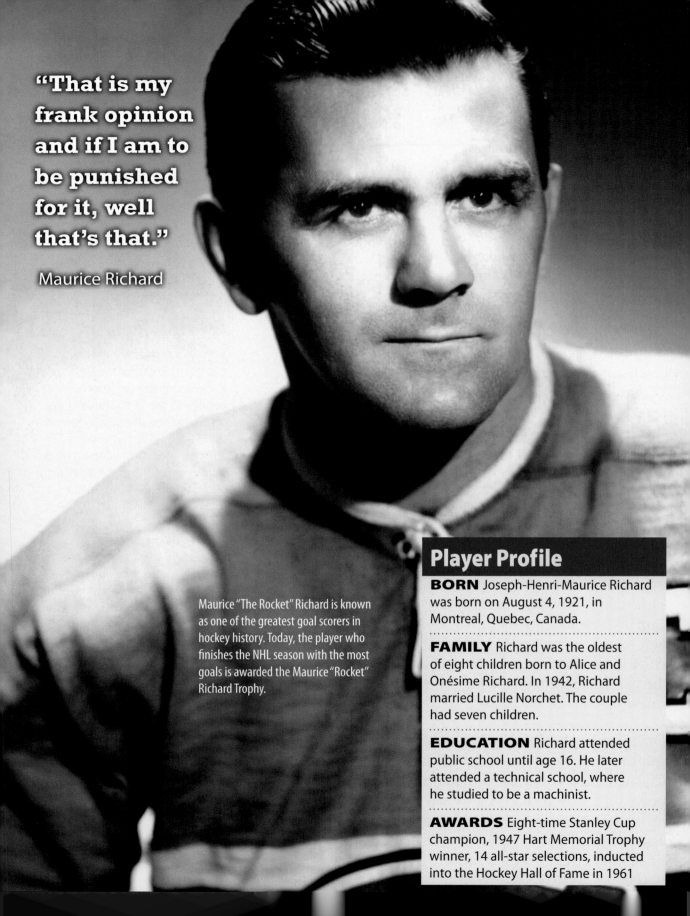

"That is my frank opinion and if I am to be punished for it, well that's that."

Maurice Richard

Maurice "The Rocket" Richard is known as one of the greatest goal scorers in hockey history. Today, the player who finishes the NHL season with the most goals is awarded the Maurice "Rocket" Richard Trophy.

Player Profile

BORN Joseph-Henri-Maurice Richard was born on August 4, 1921, in Montreal, Quebec, Canada.

FAMILY Richard was the oldest of eight children born to Alice and Onésime Richard. In 1942, Richard married Lucille Norchet. The couple had seven children.

EDUCATION Richard attended public school until age 16. He later attended a technical school, where he studied to be a machinist.

AWARDS Eight-time Stanley Cup champion, 1947 Hart Memorial Trophy winner, 14 all-star selections, inducted into the Hockey Hall of Fame in 1961

Maurice Richard

Right Wing

Early Years

Maurice Richard started playing hockey at a young age. He first played with his school team and later joined a neighborhood team. He played hockey at nearly every level in Montreal. Richard played under many different names. This way, he could play hockey for a different team each day. Richard was a fierce competitor. He suffered many injuries while playing hockey. This led many people to question if he was strong enough to play in the NHL.

Developing Skills

Richard joined the NHL's Montreal Canadiens for the 1942–1943 season. However, a broken ankle forced him off the ice after just 16 games. He came back the next season and switched his jersey number from 15 to 9. He wanted to wear number 9 in honor of his daughter, who weighed 9 pounds at birth. This season marked a turning point for Richard. He scored 54 points in 46 games. From this point on, he was one of the most dominant offensive players in the NHL.

Richard played all of his 18 NHL seasons with the Canadiens. Although he only played 978 regular season games, he scored 544 goals and had 421 assists. He also had 1,285 minutes in penalties. In 133 playoff games, Richard scored 82 goals and 44 assists. He led the Canadiens to eight Stanley Cup championships, including five in a row between 1956 and 1960. Richard scored his 500th career goal in 1957. He was the first player to ever score 500 goals. Richard retired in 1960. At the time, he held 20 NHL records, including most career goals and hat tricks.

Maurice Richard

Greatest Moment

Richard scored one of his greatest goals in the 1952 Stanley Cup semifinal versus the Boston Bruins. In the seventh and deciding game of the series, the Bruins and Canadiens were tied 1–1. Richard took a hit from a Bruins defenseman that left him dizzy and dripping blood from his face. He had to leave the game to get cleaned and bandaged.

Richard returned to the team's bench with four minutes left in the third period. After hearing the game was still tied, Richard jumped onto the ice and scored the winning goal.

In the 1944–1945 season, Maurice Richard scored 50 goals in 50 games. He was the first player ever to score 50 goals in a season.

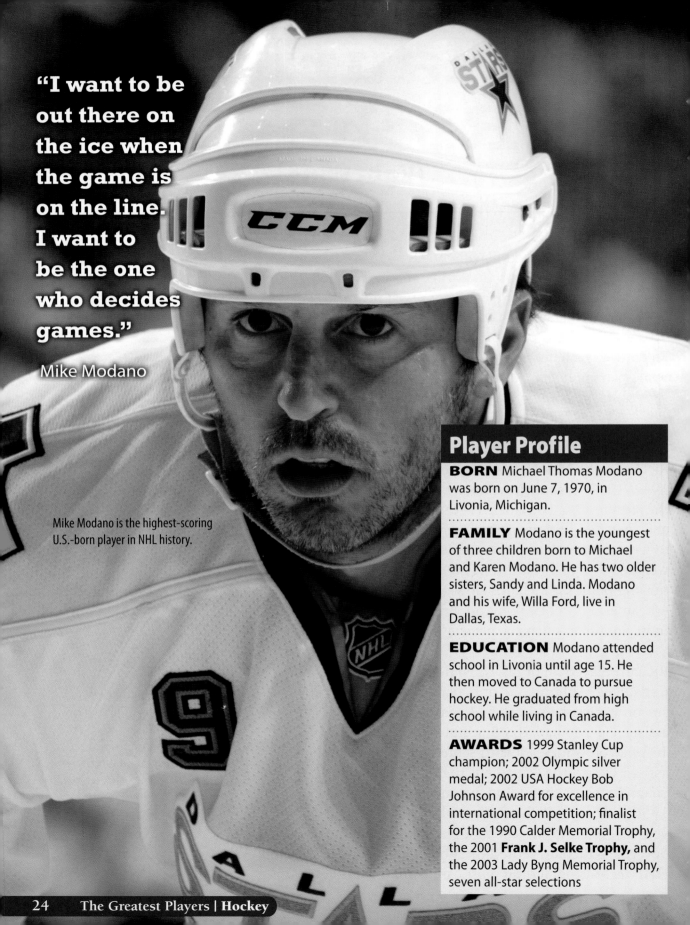

"I want to be out there on the ice when the game is on the line. I want to be the one who decides games."

Mike Modano

Mike Modano is the highest-scoring U.S.-born player in NHL history.

Player Profile

BORN Michael Thomas Modano was born on June 7, 1970, in Livonia, Michigan.

FAMILY Modano is the youngest of three children born to Michael and Karen Modano. He has two older sisters, Sandy and Linda. Modano and his wife, Willa Ford, live in Dallas, Texas.

EDUCATION Modano attended school in Livonia until age 15. He then moved to Canada to pursue hockey. He graduated from high school while living in Canada.

AWARDS 1999 Stanley Cup champion; 2002 Olympic silver medal; 2002 USA Hockey Bob Johnson Award for excellence in international competition; finalist for the 1990 Calder Memorial Trophy, the 2001 **Frank J. Selke Trophy,** and the 2003 Lady Byng Memorial Trophy, seven all-star selections

Mike Modano

Center

Early Years

Mike Modano started playing hockey at age seven. At age 15, he moved to Canada to join the Prince Alberta Raiders of the Western Hockey League. He played three seasons with the Raiders. After graduating from high school in 1988, Modano was drafted by the Minnesota North Stars.

Modano scored in his first NHL game. The 6-foot, 3-inch tall, 212-pound center played five seasons with the North Stars. In 1993, the North Stars moved to Dallas, Texas, and became the Stars. Modano's last season in Minnesota and his first season in Dallas were the two best of his career. He recorded 93 points in each of those seasons. He also scored a career-best 50 goals in the 1993–1994 season.

Developing Skills

In 1996, Modano scored a career-high four goals in one game. In the 1998–1999 season, Modano led his team to the Stanley Cup playoffs, with 81 regular-season points in 77 games played. He then added 23 points in 23 games in the playoffs on his way to winning the cup. Modano served as either team captain or alternate captain of the Stars from 1995 to 2010.

Modano played with Stars from 1993 until the end of the 2009–2010 season. During this time, he became the all-time goal-scoring and points leader for American-born players in the NHL. He also holds all of the major team scoring records for the Stars. After 21 seasons, Modano has scored 561 goals and 1,374 points. He is also in the top 30 of all-time playoff scorers, with 145 points. Brett Hull is the only American player to score more in the playoffs.

Mike Modano

Greatest Moment

Modano's hard work, speed, and goal-scoring abilities paid off on March 17, 2007. That night, he scored his 502nd and 503rd career regular season goals. With these two goals, Modano passed Joe Mullen for the most NHL goals scored by a U.S.-born player.

On November 7, 2007, Modano scored two goals in a game versus the San Jose Sharks. The second goal was his 1,233rd career point. This goal moved him ahead of Phil Housley for the all-time points record for a player born in the United States.

Mike Modano holds all of the major records for a player born in the United States, including most games played (1,499), most goals, and most points.

Greatest Moments

1959 – The Man in the Mask

When: November 1, 1959

Where: New York, New York

Montreal Canadiens goaltender Jacques Plante suffered a broken nose after a puck hit his face. The wound needed more than 200 stitches. Plante wanted to return to the ice to finish the game, but he had one condition. He had to be allowed to wear a facemask. Plante finished the game in his mask, winning 4–1. He was the first goalie in the NHL to wear a mask on a regular basis.

1970
Bobby Orr scores in overtime to win the Stanley Cup for the Boston Bruins.

1971
Jean Béliveau wins his 10th Stanley Cup.

1920   **1930**   **1940**   **1950**   **1960**

1976 – What a Night!

When: February 7, 1976

Where: Toronto, Ontario, Canada

When Toronto Maple Leafs forward Darryl Sittler laced up his skates for a home game versus the Boston Bruins, he had no idea he was about to make history. Sittler scored six goals and added four assists on his way to a record-setting 10-point game. No one before or since has managed to pull off such a feat. Even greats such as Wayne Gretzky, Mario Lemieux, and Maurice Richard only managed to tally eight points on their best nights. The Maple Leafs won the game 11–4.

1945
Maurice Richard becomes the first player to score 50 goals in 50 games.

1971
Phil Esposito sets a record with 550 shots on net, including 76 goals.

1973
Gordie Howe plays on the same line as his sons, Mark and Marty, for the Houston Aeros of the WHA.

1981 – Fastest to 50

When: December 30, 1981

Where: Edmonton, Alberta, Canada

Wayne Gretzky broke Maurice "The Rocket" Richard's record of 50 goals in 50 games when he scored five times against the Philadelphia Flyers. It was just the 39th game of the season. Richard's record had stood for 36 years. After the game, Gretzky called his dad, Walter, to tell him about the record. Walter replied, "What took you so long?" Of all the records Gretzky holds, he has said that this is the one that is least likely to be broken.

1994
Mark Messier guarantees a win for the New York Rangers in game 6 of their playoff series with the New Jersey Devils.

2007
Mike Modano becomes the highest scoring American-born player in NHL history.

2009
Martin Brodeur breaks Terry Sawchuk's record for most career shutouts.

1970 **1980** **1990** **2000** **2010**

1988
Mario Lemieux becomes the first, and only, player to score five goals in five different ways, all in the same game.

1989
Wayne Gretzky passes Gordie Howe's NHL record of 1,850 career points.

2009 – For the Win

When: March 17, 2009

Where: Newark, New Jersey

Martin Brodeur surpassed Patrick Roy for the most career wins by a goaltender. Brodeur earned his record-breaking 552nd win in a home game versus the Chicago Blackhawks. He turned aside 30 shots for a 3–2 victory. Afterward, Brodeur cut the netting off the net he defended through two periods of play that night. He then skated a victory lap around the arena.

Write a Biography

Life Story

A person's life story can be the subject of a book. This kind of book is called a biography. Biographies often describe the lives of people who have achieved great success. These people may be alive today, or they may have lived many years ago. Reading a biography can help you learn more about a great person.

Get the Facts

Use this book, and research in the library and on the Internet, to find out more about your favorite hockey player. Learn as much about this player as you can. What team did this person play for? What are his or her statistics in important categories? Has this person set any records? Be sure to also write down key events in the person's life. What was this person's childhood like? What has he or she accomplished? Is there anything else that makes this person special or unusual?

Use the Concept Web

A concept web is a useful research tool. Read the questions in the concept web on the following page. Answer the questions in your notebook. Your answers will help you write a biography.

In just six seasons, Alexander Ovechkin has set nine NHL records. He was the first player to win the Art Ross, Hart, Lester B. Pearson, and Maurice Richard trophies in the same year.

Concept Web

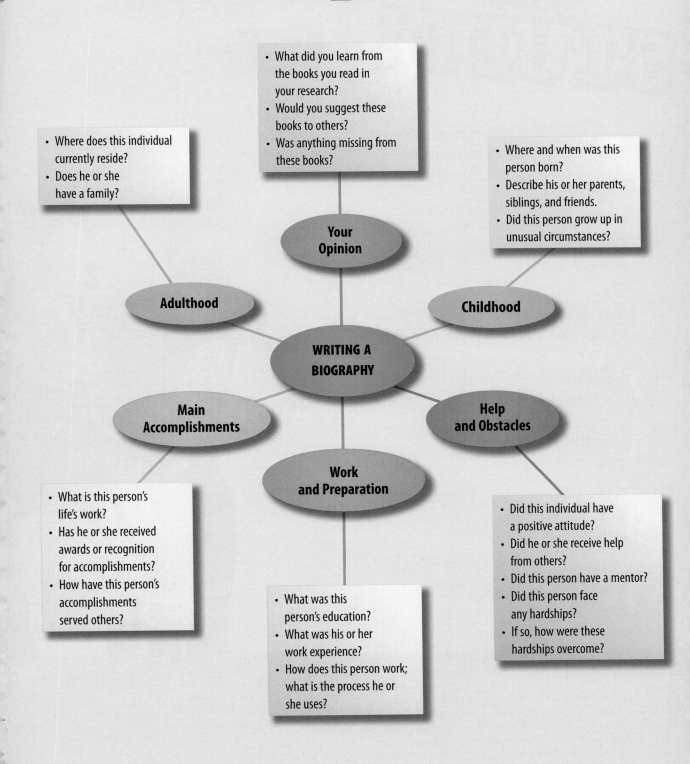

- What did you learn from the books you read in your research?
- Would you suggest these books to others?
- Was anything missing from these books?

- Where does this individual currently reside?
- Does he or she have a family?

- Where and when was this person born?
- Describe his or her parents, siblings, and friends.
- Did this person grow up in unusual circumstances?

Your Opinion

Adulthood

Childhood

WRITING A BIOGRAPHY

Main Accomplishments

Help and Obstacles

Work and Preparation

- What is this person's life's work?
- Has he or she received awards or recognition for accomplishments?
- How have this person's accomplishments served others?

- What was this person's education?
- What was his or her work experience?
- How does this person work; what is the process he or she uses?

- Did this individual have a positive attitude?
- Did he or she receive help from others?
- Did this person have a mentor?
- Did this person face any hardships?
- If so, how were these hardships overcome?

Know your STUFF!

1 Who has won the most Stanley Cups in NHL history?

2 How many shots on goal did Phil Esposito record in 1971?

3 Which of his records did Wayne Gretzky say is the least likely to be broken?

4 What is Gordie Howe's nickname?

5 How many different ways did Mario Lemieux score goals in one game?

6 Who led the New York Rangers to their first Stanley Cup championship in 54 years in 1994?

7 Bobby Orr is the only defenseman to do what?

8 The NHL's annual award for the league's top goal scorer is named after which player?

9 Who is the highest-scoring U.S.-born player in NHL history?

10 What are two records held by goaltender Martin Brodeur?

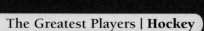

Glossary

Art Ross Trophy: an award given at the end of each NHL season to the player who has scored the most points

assists: points awarded to a player for passing the puck to a teammate who then scores a goal

Bill Masterton Memorial Trophy: an award given at the end of each NHL season to the player who best demonstrates perseverance, sportsmanship, and dedication to hockey

Calder Memorial Trophy: an award given each year to the NHL's top first year, or rookie, player

Conn Smythe Trophy: an award given each year to the player judged to be most valuable to his team during the Stanley Cup playoffs

crease: a marked area in front of each team's goal in which only the goaltender is allowed to stand

Frank J. Selke Trophy: an award given each year to the forward judged to be the best in the defensive aspects of the game

Hart Memorial Trophy: an award given each year to the player judged to be the most valuable to his team

hat trick: to score three goals in a single game

James Norris Trophy: an award given each year to the NHL's best defenseman

Lady Byng Memorial Trophy: an award given at the end of each NHL season to the player who best demonstrates sportsmanship and a high level of play

Lester B. Pearson Trophy: an award given at the end of each NHL season to the league's most outstanding player as judged by the players; renamed the Ted Lindsay Award in 2010

Major Junior: the top North American hockey league for players between the ages of 16 and 20

Most Valuable Player (MVP): the player judged to be the most valuable to his team's success

penalty shot: a free shot awarded to a player who was interfered with while attempted to take a shot on net

power play: a period of time when a team has an advantage over their opponent while an opponent player is serving a penalty

short-handed: when a team has one or more of its players serving a penalty

shutouts: games finished by a goaltender who has not allowed any goals to be scored against his or her team

Index

Log on to www.av2books.com

AV² by Weigl brings you media enhanced books that support active learning. Go to www.av2books.com, and enter the special code found on page 2 of this book. You will gain access to enriched and enhanced content that supplements and complements this book. Content includes video, audio, web links, quizzes, a slide show, and activities.

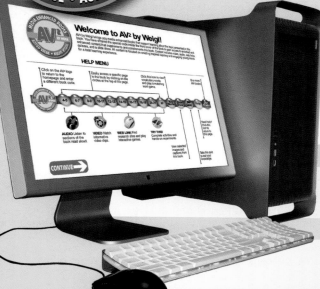

Audio
Listen to sections of the book read aloud.

Video
Watch informative video clips.

Embedded Weblinks
Gain additional information for research.

Try This!
Complete activities and hands-on experiments.

WHAT'S ONLINE?

Try This!	Embedded Weblinks	Video	EXTRA FEATURES
Try a hockey activity.	Learn more about hockey players.	Watch a video about hockey.	
Test your knowledge of hockey equipment.	Read about hockey coaches.	View stars of the sport in action.	
Complete a mapping activity.	Find out more about where hockey games take place.	Watch a video about hockey players.	

Audio
Listen to sections of the book read aloud.

Key Words
Study vocabulary, and complete a matching word activity.

Slide Show
View images and captions, and prepare a presentation.

Quizzes
Test your knowledge.

AV² was built to bridge the gap between print and digital. We encourage you to tell us what you like and what you want to see in the future.
Sign up to be an AV² Ambassador at www.av2books.com/ambassador.